95

TRAMPOLINING

Pelham Pictorial Sports Instruction Series

Cyril A. Carter
and Brian Phelps

TRAMPOLINING

 Pelham Books

First published in Great Britain by
Pelham Books Ltd
44 Bedford Square
London W.C.1
1979

ISBN 0 7207 1172 X

Filmset by Granada Graphics Ltd
and printed and bound in Great Britain by
Butler and Tanner Ltd, Frome

Contents

To my dear friends Nik Stuart, Brian Heyhurst and Robin Thomas, and all the other gymnasts and coaches who encouraged me to rise from cripple to competitor, and to my great friend Brian Jacks who had confidence in my coaching and literary ability.

'To develop a perfect human body, and have absolute control over its function, then to train it to perform acts that require courage, skill and grace . . . . What could be more basically fine than that?'

British National Gymnastic Coach
John Atkinson

Acknowledgements
Thanks are due to David Finch for the excellent photographs, and to Malcolm Hamer (Headline Enterprises Ltd) without whose efforts my work would never get into print; to Adidas (UK) Ltd for supplying sports clothing; to Ted Blake (Nissen International) for material supplied at a safety conference in 1971, and for his further advice and assistance. Plate 140 was supplied by the *Middlesex County Times*.

Foreword

It gives me great pleasure to offer a few words of introduction to this important contribution to the writings about trampolining.

Cyril Carter, Olympic gymnast, Lecturer in Human Movement Studies in the Faculty of Education at New College Durham, and also former staff coach for trampolining at the Crystal Palace National Sports Centre, has combined with Brian Phelps, Olympic diver, who became European Diving Champion at the age of 14 and overall British Trampoline Champion at the age of 15, to write this textbook during the most successful years that British competitors have experienced in world class trampolining. Although it has been specifically designed to promote the sport and recreation of trampolining amongst beginners, and is therefore invaluable for this purpose, the authors have also produced a book of worth both to the more experienced trampolinists, and to those coaches and teachers who wish to promote further success in the sport.

Perhaps the most exciting aspect of this book is the combination, in the authors, of the three major sporting aesthetic disciplines: gymnastics, diving and trampolining. Cyril, besides being a competitor in gymnastics and a coach in trampolining, has also written a recent book on highboard and springboard diving. Brian, despite not having competed as a gymnast himself, coaches many top level young gymnasts and future champions, as well as having achieved distinction as an Olympic Bronze Medallist in diving and a distinguished international career in trampolining. This powerful combination of talents will ensure for the reader that the fundamentals of this sport are adequately explained and illustrated.

Trampolining is an established international sporting event, in which Great Britain has achieved much success; it is widely practised by men, women and children of all ages nationwide. It is my sincere hope that this small volume will encourage further participation and achievement in this deeply rewarding activity.

John Davies
Director, CPNSC

Introduction

Long before Newton had an apple 'bounce' on his head, men were familiar with the limitations gravity imposed upon the human body. Man, being a perverse and stubborn sort of creature, sought many and various ways to overcome this limitation — some reasonably successful, others disastrous! But the idea of overcoming gravity, even for a second or two, stimulated the imagination of many and led them, like the early aviators, to devise ingenious contraptions by means of which their goal might be achieved.

Unlike the early aviators, however, who merely wished to emulate the birds' mastery of the air in terms of time aloft, certain men were stimulated by the potential movements that the human body could perform if only a little more time were added to the 'flight' of a normal jump — with the guarantee of a safe landing! The embryonic beginnings of such experiments may be observed in the activities of modern day young children who gain a great deal of exhilaration merely bouncing on their beds, and sometimes tossing people in blankets.

Such 'natural' activities led the early acrobats and tumblers to invent and use various devices with which to enhance their performance as entertainers. A sprung board was possibly the first of such devices, often placed across supporting blocks in order to provide a platform from which the performer might jump, and possibly return. These fifteenth century 'leapers', as they were called, often performed amazing stunts from such instruments, but clearly these were devices for the already competent tumbler. It was the circus acrobats who first came close to the concept of a trampoline, when they discovered that they got as much applause (if not more) when they landed and bounced in their safety net as when they performed a perfect stunt on the high-wire, or trapeze. Circus lore has it that one of these acrobats, named Du Trampolin, was one of the first to realise the potential of this sprung net, and subsequently went on to invent a system of spring suspension that was the forerunner of the modern-day trampoline.

It is to George Nissen, a former American diving and tumbling champion, that the modern-day trampoline owes its roots. His persistence in pioneering and constructing a properly designed machine, and in formulating proper methods of instruction in how to use it, led directly to the sport and recreation of trampolining as we know it today, and to the formation of the Nissen International Company who manufacture advanced models of his early machines.

Leaping and jumping is a natural activity spontaneously practised in play by the very young and forming an integral part of almost every virile physical education and recreation programme. It epitomizes physical fitness and the concomitant feelings of zest and well-being. Usually, however,

1.

2.

3.

4.

1–4. Mandy Phelps (aged 6), possibly one of the youngest trampolinists in the world to perform a full twisting back somersault in competition, demonstrates that trampolining is a sport, and a recreation, for all ages.

Trampolining

landing and take-off must be on and from the feet and this restricts the range of movements. Skilful tumblers can learn to fall and spring on the hands and divers can, with the springboard's helpful lift and 'soft' water landing, extend the range and complexity of these movements considerably. However, there is still some restriction and both sports demand considerable natural aptitude, special lengthy training and physical requirements for real proficiency. The trampoline enables *everyone* to master tumbling and diving movements rapidly and then, most important, to extend, develop and combine them in an almost unending variety of movement experiences possible in no other way. The skill threshold is low enough for everyone to 'get in' on the sport, yet the skill ceiling is high enough to provide scope and a challenge to the most endowed and accomplished performer.

It is not the aim of this book, nor could it ever be possible, to detail all the tricks or stunts that can be performed upon a trampoline. Our intention is to provide an outline of the performance of trampolinists, from the very basic up to the more advanced. In this manner, it is our hope that we can provide a book that will be of value both to the beginner and to the more experienced trampolinist, and also to coaches and teachers who wish to be involved in this most exciting and exhilarating sporting activity.

Cyril A. Carter
Brian Phelps

CHAPTER ONE

Preliminaries

The trampoline is, without doubt, the most exciting piece of equipment ever to have appeared on the scene of gymnastic-type activities. It has been designed in order to provide the student with greater freedom to explore the potential of body movements in flight. It provides everyone with the opportunity to perform, safely, movements which might otherwise be impossible. Like any other mechanical object that man has designed, it is only as safe as the person who uses it. The trampoline, much like a fast car in the hands of an idiot, provides equal opportunity for disaster. Just as a fast car will draw no distinction between the idiot and the competent driver, so too will the trampoline draw no distinction between novice and expert. Quite simply, whatever you put into it, it will put back at you, but with more power and speed! With this in mind, we make no apology for starting with some simple safety rules which, if observed, should guide you towards safe, enjoyable and, we hope, successful trampolining.

Safety

1. As for all sporting activities, make sure that you are properly dressed in suitable clothing: track suit, leotard, shorts, etc. It is advisable to wear proper gymnastic-type shoes for trampolining; other shoes ruin the trampoline, socks may cause you to slip, and bare feet may become painful. Remove all objects from your pockets, and from your person. Rings, watches and bracelets become lethal

5. Amusing though this comedy photograph may be, ignoring the safety rules may result in a real disaster.

objects, often to the performer, and sometimes to the coach who is supporting him.

2. Never bounce on the trampoline while alone. A minimum of five people is normally required before the trampoline should be used—one being the performer, whilst the other four stand close to each side of the trampoline in order to prevent the performer falling off. These 'spotters' should, at all times, keep their eyes on the performer, and be ready to give a supporting push if he should lose his balance sufficiently badly to come too close to the edge of the trampoline.

3. Mounting and dismounting the trampoline should be done as carefully as possible, avoiding the springs and being aware of a slippery frame or loose safety pads. Never jump from a trampoline directly onto the floor. When you are bouncing on a trampoline the muscles in your body adjust themselves to the 'soft' landing provided by the bed; attempting to jump onto the floor can therefore result in serious injury.

4. Always bounce as near to the middle of the trampoline bed as possible. If you should stray away from the centre, 'kill' your bounce, come to a halt, and walk back to the centre before starting again.

5. At all times place emphasis on control before height. It is pointless to gain great height and lose control before attempting any stunt. When attempting any new stunt work first on quality and control and build up the height gradually and safely.

6. Every new stunt should be preceded by a correct sequence of build-up movements. Make yourself aware of each stage of progress, and then master it,

before attempting the more difficult tricks. Never become impatient to attempt the next stage until you have mastered the basic foundations. Acknowledgement and observance of this rule is fundamental to success in, and enjoyment of, safe trampolining.

7. Be familiar with, and employ the use of, safety devices when learning the more advanced somersaulting movements. The overhead safety belt and the crash mat are two such devices. Make sure that the people handling this equipment for you are fully competent in its use. Never experiment with this equipment unless you have reached the correct stage in learning.

8. Until you become an experienced, and even expert, performer, do not bounce on the trampoline with another person. 'Double bouncing' is an advanced, and thus more dangerous, activity, and should be left to the expert.

9. Bouncing on the trampoline is a deceptively strenuous and tiring activity. A simple mistake caused by fatigue can often have disastrous results. Limit your time of bouncing to no more than one minute; this will avoid fatigue and give a greater number of students the chance to bounce.

10. On no account should you ever engage in any type of horseplay on, or near, a trampoline. Never use the trampoline near any area where a ball or any similar object is being used— foreign objects suddenly appearing on the trampoline may cause the performer to mistime his bounce, and end up on the floor.

Next to following the safety rules themselves, it is probably equally important, even for the expert, to perform only under the direction and supervision of a fully qualified and experienced trampoline coach. You should ensure that the person instructing you has received a suitable coaching award from the British Trampolining Federation.

Basic Mechanics

Like every other object in this universe, man is subject to certain laws of mechanics, and it is vitally important for the trampolinist to have some knowledge of the basic principles which sometimes assist, and at other times may limit, the sort of movements he can perform during his flight from the trampoline.

These laws are numerous, and often extremely complex, and we shall therefore detail only those which we feel are most important to the performer.

Gravity
The human body, like all other objects, is subject to the gravitational pull of the earth. The trampoline merely provides a limited opportunity to overcome such attraction. Simply stated, this means that 'what goes up, must come down'! The body, however, is a special kind of object, as compared to a ball or a brick, in that it can voluntarily change its shape. It should be realized that this ability to change shape voluntarily does not negate the other laws of mechanics. It may be comforting to realize, however, that should you fall over a cliff then you may choose whether to land completely stretched out or tucked up like a ball. No brick can do that. Nor can a ball!

Centre of Gravity
All objects possess a centre of gravity. In a perfectly even-shaped object, like a ball, that centre of gravity will be located exactly in the middle. In an object as fluid as man, however, the centre of gravity varies with the position and the shape of the individual. Simply stated, the centre of gravity is the imaginary point about which the weight and distribution of all parts of the body are equally located. In general, for a man standing upright with both hands at his side, the centre of gravity will be located slightly below his navel, and at a point directly above his feet. Should our man bend at the waist, whilst maintaining his balance, his centre of gravity will be located outside his body, but still directly over his feet. This may appear to be a difficult concept to understand, but it will become more apparent to the performer as he gains experience of the more difficult stunts.

Action, Reaction
Isaac Newton's 'Third Law of Motion' states: 'for every action there is an equal and opposite reaction'. For the trampolinist this means, quite simply, that the amount of effort you put into the trampoline, and the manner in which it is done, will be reflected in the amount of height you will gain and the manner and direction in which you will travel. This law also has its effect on the type of movements that are performed when in the air: if an arm is swung vigorously outwards from the body, the result will be that the body will attempt to spin in the opposite direction.

Rotation and Gyration
Man has long known the challenge of performing 'gyration' with his own body during its flight through the air as a

13

projectile. It is natural, therefore, that this area of performance should claim the most attention in any writings on trampolining. 'Rotation' refers to that action where the body turns around an imaginary pole or line that stretches from one side of the body to the other (eg as in any forward or backward rolling action or somersaults). 'Gyration' refers to that action when the body turns (or spins) around an imaginary line running from the top of the head through to the soles of the feet (e.g. any pirouetting or twisting activity). When a trampolinist has started to perform either of these actions, and whilst he is still up in the air, he may choose to speed up or slow down such movements by altering the shape of his body. To speed up a somersaulting movement he may tuck up into a tight ball; alternatively, stretching out straight will slow down such rotation. Similarly, when he gyrates or twists, extending the arms out sideways will slow down the move-ment, whilst pulling the arms in close to his body will cause the movement to speed up. It should be noted, however, that he can never reverse the direction of his somersault or twist once it has started and whilst still in the air.

In concluding this difficult but necessary section on basic mechanics it is also necessary to make some mention of the path of the centre of gravity. Quite simply, once we have lost contact with the trampoline bed nothing can be done to alter the path along which the body will travel. No movements that we can per-form whilst up in the air will provide greater or lesser height or distance. We can alter the shape of our body around the centre of gravity, but this will not alter the amount of spring we received from the trampoline, nor the direction in which this spring has been set. Thus, if we make a mistake at take-off there is very little we can do to alter the situation—except to choose the sort of shape our body will assume upon landing!

Fundamental Bouncing

'Checking' or Stopping the Bounce (Plates 6–7)

Unlike most other sports, before you ever begin trampolining it is first necessary that you should learn how to stop—bouncing that is! This is rather like first learning to ride a bicycle; if you don't know how to apply the brakes, then you are going to be in a great deal of trouble should something unexpected happen and you wish to stop quickly! So, too, it is vitally important that the beginner should know how to 'check' his bounce, in preparation for those times when he loses control or strays too far away from the centre of the trampoline.

The most common method of checking the bounce is by using a 'knee-break' stop, where the performer absorbs the rebound of the trampoline by bending at the knees, much in the same manner as a skier absorbs any bumps in the snow. From a low and controlled bounce, practise absor-bing the force of the jump by bending at the knees just at the point where the feet make contact with the bed. At this point the knees remain relaxed and slightly bent in order to absorb any rebound force that remains, and the feet remain in firm contact with the bed until all movement has stopped. The arms extend forwards and outwards in order to help maintain

6–7. *Knee break stop. Notice how the knees are bent to absorb the force of the landing when the feet contact the bed.*

good balance. If performed correctly, this method provides an immediate and graceful finish to all bouncing.

Bouncing (Plates 8–9)

The key to all good trampolining is the mastery of perfect, controlled bouncing, before attempting any of the more difficult stunts. First, you must learn to perform

8–9. *Initiating the bounce. The combination of a good straight arm swing with the feet depressing the bed results in a strong initial lift into the jump.*

straight bouncing from feet to feet. Stand in the middle of the trampoline, with the feet approximately shoulder width apart in order to aid stability. Focus the eyes on the frame pad at the end of the trampoline. To start the bounce, lift the arms upwards and to the side, and rise up on to your toes. Rotate the arms backwards and swing them downwards, whilst bending at the knees

Trampolining

and waist. As the arms swing downwards, the heels come in contact with the bed, and the hips and knees are forcefully straightened, in order to depress the bed downwards in preparation for the jump.

As the bed begins to recoil, the arms swing straight forward and upwards, combining with a push downwards with the toes, whilst the body is held tense and reasonably straight. As you lose contact with the bed, the arms continue to swing upward and the feet are brought together, with the toes fully pointed. At the top of the jump, where the performer 'floats' momentarily, the arms relax and rotate slightly backwards in preparation for the descent and landing. As you land, bring the arms backwards to a position where their upward swing can be repeated in the next bounce. On contact with the bed, control the bend of the knees and hips. The feet should flatten on contact with the bed, and resume a position approximately shoulder width apart. Extension of the knees and hips combined with a swing of the arms will result in a further bounce.

In the early stages, it is vital to concentrate on controlling all movements of the body in the air in order that you can be confident of a safe and correct landing. It is also vital that you establish a habit of performing all bounces in the centre of the trampoline ('spotting the bounce'); if any movement away from the centre should occur, stop and walk back, before beginning to bounce again.

Basic Jumps (Plates 10–14)
Apart from straight bouncing, there are four other basic jumps which will aid the student in mastering control of his body in the air. The first two of these, tucked and piked jumps, combined with the straight jump, illustrate the basic fundamental positions in which somersaults are later to be performed. Straight jumping with a half, or more, twist, serves to introduce the performer to a technique which, when combined with somersaults, will later result in the performance of the more spectacular and extremely complex stunts. The last of these, the straddle jump, is a further variation of the piked jump which helps the beginner to add variety to his basic performance.

It is as well to begin by performing these positions either sitting on, or by jumping off, the floor; this will give you some of the necessary 'feel' of the type of balance involved, before subjecting the movement to the degree of lift provided by the trampoline.

After completing the leg drive, the tucked jump is achieved, by bending at the knees and waist so that the upper leg contacts the chest. The hands momentarily clasp the shins, with the elbows being held close to the body. The piked jump is similar except that the legs remain perfectly straight and together, whilst the body bends sharply at the waist to meet the legs as they are raised. The hands may either make contact with the feet, or be held straight out to the side. The straddle jump is merely a piked jump with the legs being held wide apart: the hands may either contact the feet or alternatively reach down between the performer's legs. All these positions are achieved at the very peak of the bounce, and should be released in a controlled manner in order to achieve the correct position for further bouncing.

In order to perform a half-twist jump, the

11.

12.

13.

10–14. These plates demonstrate the basic body positions achieved in the fundamental jumps and, apart from the straddle jump, show clearly the body shapes in which the later somersaults will be performed.

10. Straight jump.
11. Tuck jump.
12. Pike jump.
13. Straddle jump. In this photograph the performer is about to make contact with his hands

14.

upon his feet; alternatively, the arms may be swung down between the legs. In either case the body should fold as deeply as for the piked jump.
14. Full twist jump.

17

Trampolining

performer slightly turns the shoulders and the head, in the direction he wishes to turn, at the point immediately prior to the feet losing contact with the bed. The body is held perfectly straight, and the arms may be either pulled close in against the chest or extended upwards, in line with the body. Looking to the left results in a turn to the left; looking right, a turn to the right. The harder the force of the turn and the quicker and tighter the 'wrap' of the arms, the greater the amount of twist, viz: full-twist, one-and-a-half twist, double-twist, etc.

Common Faults. The majority of faults that occur in the basic jumps are usually as a result of an incorrect take-off, resulting in a loss of balance in the air. Lack of body

tension and control may also hinder the execution of these jumps. As with all trampolining, the performer should have a clear idea of what is expected in these stunts.

There are many other methods by which twisting movements are initiated, but the performer will become more familiar with these when he starts to execute twisting somersaults.

All of these basic jumps should be performed smoothly, without loss of balance, and without loss of 'form'. Having mastered them, the performer should then attempt to execute all these jumps in 'swing-time', consecutively, using as many different combinations as possible, without loss of height or control.

CHAPTER TWO

Basic Exercises

Fundamental Landing Forms

Unlike gymnastics and diving, where the majority of take-offs and landings occur with either the hands or feet, the trampoline provides a greater, and safer, opportunity for variation. Generally, there are five other recognized landing positions from which the performer may choose to land and bounce: knees, seat, hands and knees, front, and back. Not only do they provide a novel experience for the beginner, and an opportunity to expand his repertoire, they also serve to enhance the safety aspect with regard to the performance of more difficult stunts. The gymnast who commits himself to the performance of a double-back somersault has no alternative but to land on his feet; if it should go wrong, then he will be lucky to escape injury. This is not true for a trampolinist, who may choose to land in one of several positions should he need to, and with a great deal more time for selection! Some of these landing forms are even used by the more experienced trampolinists from which to perform more advanced techniques and, therefore, it is vital that they should be mastered before moving on to somersaults.

Knee Drop (Plate 15)

Using a normal straight-bounce, the performer merely bends his knees at right-angles immediately prior to landing. The knees should start to bend upon coming down, and complete their bend just before the point of contact with the bed. Although the body may bend slightly at the waist, it is vitally important to keep body tension. The landing is achieved, simultaneously, on the knees, shins and insteps of the feet. Be careful not to arch the back.

15. Knee drop. Note the upright, and slightly piked, body position. In this photograph the arms are in a perfect position to drive upwards out of the bounce.

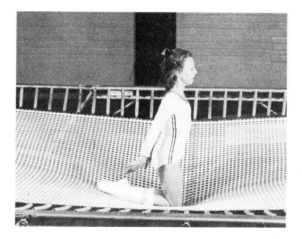

Trampolining

Common Faults. Excessive bending at the waist, together with loss of body tension, may result either in collapsing of the body when contacting the bed or, alternatively, slight forward rotation when attempting to retain the feet. Any arching of the back may cause recovery to the feet to be extremely difficult, due to slight backward rotation—arching of the back, in this stunt, can cause injury and should thus be avoided.

Seat Drop (Plate 16)
After a preliminary bounce, and at the point of take-off, the hips are pushed slightly forward, causing the shoulders to be pulled slightly backwards. Just at the point where the performer begins to descend, the hips flex and the legs are raised, but are kept straight. Raising the legs causes the head and shoulders to move slightly forward. The hands are brought down to a position slightly behind the hips, palm downwards and with the fingers pointing forwards. A controlled bending at the waist

16. Seat drop. In this landing the legs are held perfectly straight, whilst the hands are placed on the bed with the fingers pointing forwards and the arms slightly flexed, in order to provide a strong push back up to the feet.

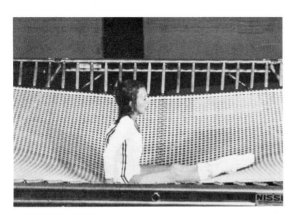

will result in a simultaneous contact of the hands, seat and legs with the bed. With correct tension in the upper body and the legs, the upward spring, combined with a slight push of the hands, will allow the performer to return to his feet by straightening at the waist.

Common Faults. The most common fault in the seat drop is to make contact either with the heels or with the seat before any other part of the legs. It is important that contact with the seat and the heels be simultaneous. Failure to push the hips forward slightly upon take-off may result in the body assuming an excessively deep piked position, causing recovery to the feet to become difficult. Incorrect hand positioning may result in a failure to provide an adequate push, and subsequent rotation, in order to lower the legs for subsequent foot bounce.

Up until this point, the upper body has remained virtually upright throughout all of the techniques. It should be noted that from this point onwards varying degrees of rotation (somersaulting) will occur, and that the following basic landings involve an introduction to basic controlled rotation, vital to the confidence and execution of the somersaults which will follow.

Hands and Knees Drop (Plate 17)
Just prior to losing contact with the bed, the hips are lifted gently, upwards and backward, causing the shoulders and head to rotate forwards and downwards during the jump. This gentle rotation continues during the descent towards the bed, when the waist and knees are bent at right angles. The arms reach forward

17. Hands and knees drop. Firm contact must be made with the bed simultaneously with hands and knees, whilst the back remains parallel to the trampoline.

18. Front drop. In this photograph we can see clearly that the arms are folded in front of the face, and that the legs are slightly flexed in preparation to drive back up to the upright position.

and downwards towards a position upon which the eyes are focused. Contact is made simultaneously with the knees and hands, but not with the insteps. At the point of contact the back should be parallel to the trampoline, with the head held naturally. A push with the hands, combined with the lift of the bed, will return the performer up onto his feet.

Common Faults. Failure to achieve the correct amount of rotation may cause contact with the bed to be made prematurely by either the hands or the knees. The performer must ensure that sufficient rotation is initiated so that his back is parallel with the bed immediately prior to contact. There may also be a tendency to jump forwards into this drop; this must be resisted by lifting the hips slightly upwards and backwards, so that the trick is 'spotted' on the centre of the trampoline.

Front Drop (Plate 18)
The take-off for front drop is performed in

exactly the same manner as for hands and knees drop. As the performer descends from his semi-tucked position he extends his body and, at the same time, brings the arms up to a position where they are sharply bent with the elbows pointing out sideways, level with the shoulders. This movement is timed in such a way as to ensure a firm contact on the bed with the hands, forearms, chest, abdomen and thighs, simultaneously. With the body held rigid on landing, a return to the feet is effected by pushing with the hands and straightening the legs, when the trampoline rebounds. (Although we have described the basic front drop, it should be noted that it may be performed with either a tucked, piked or straight entry phase.)

The best method of learning the front drop is by performing two consecutive hands and knees drops, without returning to the feet and keeping the back parallel to the bed. Then repeat, but, whilst in the air, just prior to the second hands and knees drop, extend the legs and

21

arms into the correct position for front drop.

Common Faults. Apart from jumping forward into the techique, as for the hands and knees drop, one of the most common faults is an excessive arching of the back immediately prior to contact. If this is combined with either excessive or insufficient rotation, then damage to the back may occur. It is vitally important, therefore, that the hands and knees drop is mastered before this stunt is attempted.

Back Drop (Plate 19)
The arms are swung upwards, and the hips are pushed gently forwards and upwards upon take-off, causing the body to rotate gently backwards. The chin is held well in against the chest, and the eyes focus forward on the frame of the trampoline. As the performer begins to descend, the knees are flexed and drawn slightly upwards towards the chest. Just prior to landing the legs are straightened, whilst the arms are held straight out in front of the chest. The rotation should be just sufficient for the performer to contact the bed with the upper part and middle of his back. At no time should the back of the head come in contact with the trampoline. In order to regain the upright position, the performer begins to open out at the waist by pushing the hips gently forwards and legs downwards, immediately before the back loses contact with the bed, straightening out completely before landing. (As with the front drop, this stunt may be performed with a tucked, piked or straight entry and exit; unlike the front drop, it may also be performed with a hollow, or arched, entry and exit.)

19. Back drop. In this photograph, it can be seen clearly that the back makes a firm contact with the bed whilst the arms and legs are held straight out in front of the body. It should be noted that the performer's eyes are focusing forward upon her legs, and that the back of the head does not make contact with the trampoline.

Common Faults. Insufficient rotation, often due to fear of falling backwards, results in the performer making contact with the seat rather than the upper part of the back. Failure to lift the legs into a sufficiently piked position will often result in failure to regain the feet. On no account should the performer throw his head backwards; it should be stressed that the chin is held against the chest throughout the initial stages of learning.

Twisting the Basics

Having mastered the basic drops, the student may then proceed to add a half twist, either upon entry or upon exit, or both, during the performance of the same stunt. Although all of the basic drops can be performed with the addition of one or two separate half twists, we have chosen to illustrate only two of the many techniques: half twist to back drop and half twist to front drop, from and to the feet.

21.

22.

20.

20–2. Half twist to back drop. In plate 20 the performer has initiated the twist whilst the body is held in a straight position, in order to achieve a perfectly controlled back drop landing.

Half Twist to Back Drop (Plates 20–22)
The take-off for this movement is almost the same as for front drop (i.e. the twist does not start until after the feet have left the bed). Soon after initiating the take-off, the arms assume a wide position, whilst the upper body rotates slightly forward, as for front drop. As the performer begins to descend, the right arm (if the twist is to the left) initiates a wide sweeping action down towards the right knee in order to initiate the twist. As the body twists, the eyes are focused upon the bed, until the action is well under way. The action is completed by continuing the sweep of the right arm, turning the head, and piking at the waist to assume the correct position for a back drop landing. Recovery from the back is the same as for back drop. One way of interpreting this movement is as a late twisting front drop, where the arm-sweep causes a back drop landing.

Common Faults. The most common fault in this technique is the attempt to initiate the twist far too early, and whilst the feet are still in contact with the bed. This often results in a lack of rotation or, at best, an untidy and off-balance back drop landing. It is vital that the performer achieve a front drop position in the air before initiating the twist.

23

23. *This photograph demonstrates perfectly the straight body position that should be maintained throughout the performance of this stunt, until reaching a front drop landing. The turn has been executed to the performer's left, resulting in a front drop landing with the performer's head at the right side of the picture.*

Half Twist to Front Drop (Plate 23)
The take-off for this movement is similar to that for a seat drop (i.e. with not as much backward rotation as for a back drop where the legs rotate nearly 180° from standing). The hips are pushed strongly forward with a slight twist in the direction you wish to turn, whilst shoulders lean back and turn in the same direction. With the turn having been initiated, the body and legs are held perfectly straight, the head still facing in the original direction. The head and shoulders continue to turn, while the body is still rotating, until the performer is almost face-on to the bed. At this point a slight flex of the hips may be used in order to adjust for a good front drop landing. After initiating suitable rotation, it is vital that a straight body position

be assumed throughout the rest of the turn.

Common Faults. The greatest danger in this technique is over-rotation, causing the front drop to land with the hands and chest first. The stunt must first be performed to hands and knees drop, placing emphasis upon performing only a slight amount of rotation — not as much as for a normal back drop.

Having mastered the art of putting a half twisting movement onto the basic landing positions, the student may now proceed to move from a basic landing position, performing a half twist into a repeat of the same movement—as in the movement from seat drop, half twist directly into seat drop, without a foot bounce in between.

Swivel-Hips (Seat, Half Twist to Seat) (Plates 24–7)
The first part of this stunt is the same as for a normal seat drop landing. As the trampoline begins to recoil, give a strong push with the hands to initiate a slightly greater rotation than would be required to return to feet. As you begin to rise upwards, raise the arms up over the head and turn the shoulders and trunk in the desired direction of twist. Straighten at the waist, so that at the highest point your body is fully stretched and has performed a quarter (90°) turn. Continue to turn, dropping the arms and piking at the waist in order to land in a seat drop, facing in the opposite direction. A return to the feet is achieved in the same manner as for a normal seat drop.

Common Faults. A failure to achieve a

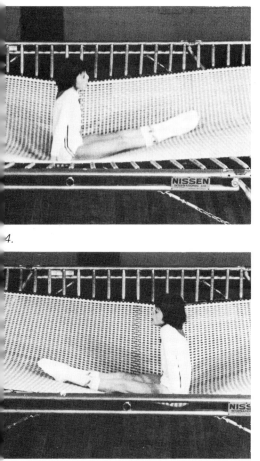

4.

7.

25.

26.

24–7. Swivel hips. In these photographs it is important to note the straight and upright body position, with the arms being held above the head, throughout the performance of the twist.

vertically upright position during the twist results in the performer attempting to remain in a piked position, and bringing his legs around the side. This must be corrected by performing a seat drop half twist to feet, followed immediately by another seat drop.

Advanced Twisting

Progression from this point onwards is normally combined with the learning of somersaults, having now achieved all of the movements necessary to safer advanced trampolining. The student may, however, go on to perform greater amounts of twist (i.e. full, one-and-a-half, double, etc.) into and out of the basics in order to be prepared for the multiple-twisting somersaults which occur later during the more advanced somersaults. It must be stressed that there are numerous twisting variations for the basics, and that we have selected only one: full twist, back to back.

28.

29.

Cat Twist (Full Twist, Back Drop to Back Drop) (Plates 28–33)

After performing the normal back drop it is vital that no forward rotation should be initiated, in order to be able to return to back drop after twisting. It is also vital that the body be in a straight position in order to be able to twist efficiently. Therefore, the student should first perform a back drop, un-piking to open out to a straight position in the air before returning to a back drop on the same spot. Having mastered this particular movement the performer is now ready to perform a full twist at the point where the body opens out straight. Having performed a drop onto the back, the performer lifts his body to a straight position, but with a strong turn of the hips in the desired direction of twist. The arms are generally kept in line with the body in order to aid the twist, whilst the head turns, first to look at the trampoline, completing the turn before the body pikes to assume a normal back drop position, before returning back up to feet.

Common Faults. After the performance of the first back drop, a common mistake is the failure to extend the legs upwards in order to achieve a straight body position for the execution of the twist; quite often the performer will attempt to execute the twist whilst in a piked position or, alternatively, will execute the same action of the legs as if attempting to return to feet. The latter results in the failure to achieve the second back drop. It should be noted that any attempt to initiate the twist too early will result in the performer travelling sideways across the bed. It is therefore important for the performer to master the back drop, opening out to a straight position, and returning to a back drop.

Routines

Trampolining is all about routines; the consecutive performance of two or more stunts without any free bounces. Having mastered only a few of the basics, the beginner should be encouraged to link them together in one controlled and continuous performance. Not only will this increase his enjoyment in the activity, but it will also aid his learning by putting him into situations where he is forced to think out, and remember, a lot more of what he is trying to achieve.

Competitive trampolining consists in the performance of ten separate stunts in swing-time. All routines are judged, like gymnastics and diving, on the basis of form, control, continuity, beauty, style and freedom from errors. Although different movements are awarded different marks, depending upon the degree of difficulty involved, difficulty and daring should at no time be confused with recklessness! A

26

30.

31.

32.

28–33. Cat twist. This series of photographs demonstrates perfectly the reason why this technique is so named. Note in plate 31 the perfectly straight body position so vital to any good twisting action.

33.

routine should contain only those stunts which the performer has already mastered, and not those of which he is unsure, or that are unsafe. The following routine comprises the basic stunts examined up to this point, successful completion of which would qualify the performer for the elementary Bronze Award of the British Trampoline Federation.

10 Contact Routine
1. Seat drop
2. Half twist to seat drop
3. Half twist to feet
4. Jump with half twist
5. Tuck jump
6. Front drop
7. To feet
8. Piked straddle jump
9. Back drop
10. To feet

CHAPTER THREE

Basic Somersaults

There is no doubt at all that one of the most exciting times in any performer's career is when he first learns to somersault in the air. From the initial feelings of terror to the joy of the first successful solo performance, the trampolinist first discovers the complete range of emotions that is provided by this sport. It is this very process which inspires many to achieve mastery of the more complex techniques, acting rather like a drug on the nervous system, providing feelings of both fear and elation. Like the use of any beneficial drug, it should be experienced only in small doses. Progress in trampolining should be slow enough to avoid too much fear, but fast enough to provide constant sources of elation.

The sport of trampolining is all about what happens up in the air. The types of take-off and landing, when properly mastered, become incidental to the grace and beauty of any performance; they are of technical concern only to the performer and his coach. It is for these reasons that the initial experience and mastery of basic somersaults is vitally important. Any imperfections that occur at this stage may later result in fear and failure (and possibly

danger) during the more advanced stages.

There are several ways in which to learn the basic somersaults, and the best way depends entirely upon the existing movement skills of the individual performer. Some take to somersaults 'like ducks to water', whilst others take greater time in building up the necessary confidence and skill. No matter which method is chosen, it is correct only if it leads to the achievement of a safe, enjoyable and technically correct performance, which will allow for the mastery of more complex skills.

Forward Rotation

This is normally the first direction in which somersaults are learned, possibly because there is less fear involved in rotating forwards. Nevertheless, it is made more difficult than backward rotation because the performer is usually 'blind' upon landing. Forward rotation should already have been experienced through the correct performance of a front drop, prior to any attempt at the performance of the front somersault.

35.

34–6. Front somersault. Strong backward and upward hip lift has initiated enough rotation for the performer to extend his legs quickly into a shallow pike and subsequently to a good 'out' position.

36.

The most important part of any forward rotation is the type of hip lift that is used in order to initiate the movement. After describing the performance of a front somersault, we shall briefly detail those movements which help the performer to 'lead up', safely, to the complete stunt. Essentially, the action of the hips is the same as for the front drop, the difference being mainly in the degree of rotation, and in the method of take-off and/ or landing.

Front Somersault (Tucked) (Plates 34–6)
Having initiated the bounce, using the normal arm action, the performer thrusts his hips upwards and slightly backwards in an effort to initiate forward rotation. This action causes the body to flex at the waist, forcing the head and shoulders forward into the rotation. At the highest

point, and with the body already rotating, the arms are brought sharply downwards to make contact with the shins, which have assumed a tucked position. This action, combined with a ducking of the head, speeds up the rotation in order to facilitate a full somersault. At the point where the somersault is almost three-quarters completed, and where the face is pointing directly at the ceiling, a positive kick out is executed in order to provide for a safe landing. The kick out is performed by straightening the legs, and un-piking at the waist with the arms extending side-ways or up above the head so that the body is in a completely open position. Because the landing is 'blind' it is essential, especially in the early stages, to emphasize a positive action out of the tuck position in order to prevent the dangers of over-rotating or landing in an unbalanced

29

position. With practice this landing will be executed with very little difficulty, but it is important to emphasize that the eyes must be kept open even though nothing may be consciously observed by the performer.

It is unusual for any performer to place a front somersault at any point in a routine other than at the end. This is because it is extremely difficult to come from a 'blind' landing into another stunt with a good degree of certainty that the next stunt will not be affected.

Progressive Stages for Front Somersault
(a)   Tucked forward roll, either on the floor or on the trampoline.
(b)   Knee drop, three-quarters forward turn-over to back drop (controlled).
(c)   Knee drop, turn-over to seat drop.
(d)   Foot bounce, tucked three-quarters turn-over to back drop (controlled).
(e)   Front somersault (supported).
(f)   Front somersault (unsupported).

Each of these stages should be performed with sufficient height and control, before progressing onto the next stage. If any breakdown in performance should occur, return immediately to the last stage where success was achieved.

Common Faults. Faults in rotation often occur as a result of an insufficient, or mistimed hip lift. Too early usually results in low but fast rotation. Too late usually results in high but slow rotation. It is important that the hip lift should be correctly timed, and of sufficient strength to provide the correct amount of rotation. Travelling forward, in the direction of the somersault, is often a result of throwing the head and arms downwards, rather than lifting the hips upwards and backwards, in order to achieve somersault rotation. Travelling backwards ('gaining'), in the opposite direction to the somersault, is often a result of excessive backward hip lift. The latter may, initially, be regarded as a 'good fault' in that it is less dangerous than forward travel, although it is still undesirable and should be corrected.

Front Somersault (Piked) (Plates 37–42)
Prior to executing the piked front somersault it is important that the performer should be able to execute a high, and controlled, tucked front somersault. This is because the action of piking produces slower rotation than that of tucking the body up tightly. Using the same initial take-off as for the tucked front somersault, but with a much stronger hip lift, the performer bends sharply at the waist whilst keeping the legs perfectly straight, and with the toes held pointed. The head and chest close tightly towards the knees whilst the hands grasp behind the knees to facilitate a tightly piked position. The landing is executed at the same point as for the tucked somersault except that the legs remain straight throughout. Once again, it is important to note that the performer should execute a positive movement from the piked to the extended position, in order to prevent the possibility of over-rotating.

Common Faults. Apart from the usual faults that occur in front somersaulting, the most common faults are failure to achieve sufficient hip lift and/or sufficient piking at the waist, in order to achieve enough rotation.

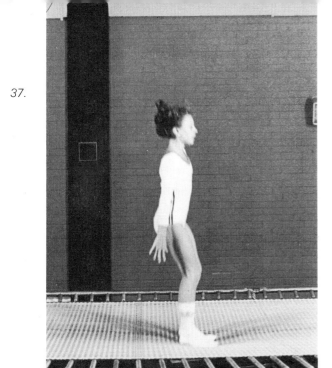
37.

38.

39.

40.

41.

42.

37–42. Front somersault (piked). Erica Phelps (aged 11), a Great Britain Youth International, provides a perfect illustration of this technique. Note the superbly tight piked position achieved in plate 40, allowing for high and controlled take-off and landing phases.

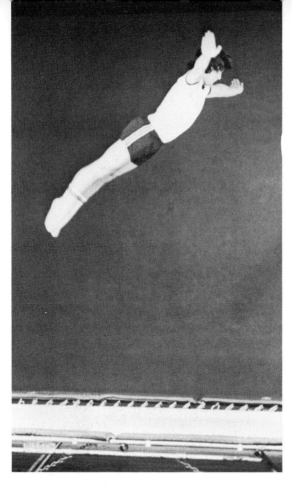

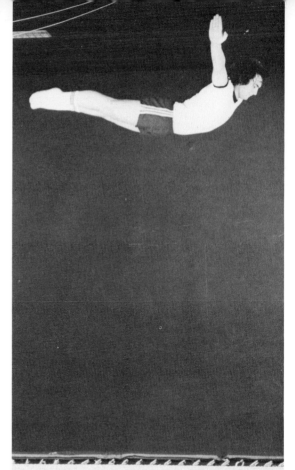

43.

44.

'Crash Dive' (Straight Three-Quarters Front Somersault to Piked Back Drop Landing) (Plates 43–7)

In this technique the performer intends to initiate only that rotation sufficient to execute half a somersault (180° rotation), with the body being held in a straight or extended position. The take-off is initiated in the same manner as for a high front somersault, except that the hip lift is far less exaggerated and the heels lift backwards in the air, in order to achieve a straight body position as quickly as possible. Throughout the majority of the rotation the head is held up, looking towards the centre of the bed, and the arms are extended forwards and slightly sideways. The performer aims to maintain the

extended body position as long as possible, and does not duck the head under and pike at the waist until the last second. This action, performed late, results in a normal piked back drop landing where the performer may easily regain his feet. It should be noted that this technique should be performed only by those trampolinists who have the necessary experience and confidence, in order to provide for safety. Initially, it may be performed into a crash mat, in which case it is vitally important to emphasize the ducking of the chin onto the chest immediately prior to landing in the back drop position.

Common Faults. Two major faults can occur in this technique. The first is due to

45.

46.

47.

the fact that insufficient heel lift is initiated in order to achieve a straight body position throughout the technique; this often results in over-rotation to a seat drop landing. The second is a failure to maintain the straight body position, and ducking the head too early, which results once again in over-rotation.

Backward Rotation

Backward rotation may be regarded as being technically more simple to perform than forward rotation. This is because, in backward rotation, the performer has a clear sight of the bed upon landing —unless, of course, he chooses to land in a back drop position. The greatest

43–7. Crash dive (three-quarters front somersault straight). Paul Burgoine, ranked second in the World Age Group Championships in 1971, displays good flight after the initial heel lift into this movement. Notice that the head ducks under only at the last minute to assume a perfect back drop landing.

33

48.

49.

inhibitor to backward rotation is fear, mainly because this is a more unnatural direction in which the body is used to travelling in safety. It may be noted that the majority of children do not respond to this fear as readily as adults; it is important, however, for the performer to have already executed backward rotation in terms of the back drop.

Back Somersault (Tucked) (Plates 48–52)
Using a natural arm action, the performer lifts from the bed, simultaneously initiating a thrust of the hips in a forward and upward direction, in a similar manner to the action of a high back drop, except with greater force. This action causes the head and shoulders to rotate backwards as the performer is lifting into the air. It should be noted that the performer never leans his head or upper body backwards as if to execute a gymnastic back flip. Having

achieved a stretched position, the performer increases rotation by bending at the knees and waist, whilst dropping the hands, to assume a tucked position. The head may either be carried in a 'natural' position or, alternatively, may aid rotation by looking sharply backwards, when the tuck position is assumed. Having performed a three-quarters rotation (270°), and at the point where the performer gains sight of the bed, the legs are extended sharply so that the body achieves a straight position—although in the initial stages the tuck may be retained slightly later due to lack of height or rotation. In this manner rotation is controlled, and the performer may adjust his landing in order to be able to execute any further stunt he requires.

Progressive Stages for Back Somersault
(a)   Tucked backward roll, either on the

34

50.

51.

floor or on the trampoline.

(b) Back drop (controlled).
(c) Loose back drop, with the legs held high, back pull-over to hands and knees (controlled).
(d) Back pull-over, increasing height to land on the knees or on the feet.
(e) Back somersault (supported).
(f) Back somersault (unsupported).

Common Faults. As with the front somersault (tucked), similar faults in rotation may occur through incorrect or insufficient hip lift at the start of the technique, resulting in low but fast rotation, or high and slow rotation. The most common fault, however, is to throw back the head, and thus the shoulders, at take-off, thus causing excessive backward travel along the bed. This must be corrected by emphasizing the thrust of the hips forwards and upwards at take-off.

52.

48–52. Back somersault (tucked). Allison Stuart (aged 11), also a Great Britain Youth International, and National Schools Champion in 1978, demonstrates the vital hip lift necessary to the performance of this technique, and a perfectly controlled straight body position in preparation for her landing.

54.

55.

53–5. Back somersault (piked). Once again, Erica Phelps demonstrates her superb mastery of piked techniques. It should be noted that the piked position is assumed only after the trampolinist has left the bed, and then with great speed (compare plates 53 and 54).

53.

Back Somersault (Piked) (Plates 53–5)
The take-off for this somersault is initiated in the same manner as for the tucked back somersault, except that the performer initiates a far stronger forward and upward hip thrust. Immediately after leaving the bed, the legs are snapped forwards and upwards towards the chest, whilst being held perfectly straight and together. The hands clasp the legs firmly, at a point just behind the knees, causing the rotation to speed up considerably. The landing is executed in the same way as the tucked somersault, except that the performer merely unpikes at the waist to assume a straight position immediately prior to descending towards the bed.

Back Somersault (Straight) (Plates 56–9)
This somersault is executed in much the same way as the piked back somersault, except that the performer initiates a stronger hip thrust in order to provide enough rotation to execute the complete somersault with the body being held in a straight, controlled position. Prior to modern-day trampolining, this somersault would have been executed with a hollow or arched back; for the modern-day technique the performer controls his body tension in order to execute the technique as a straight somersault.

56.

57.

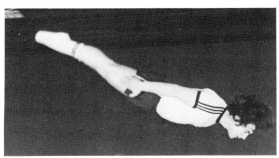

58.

Common Faults. Apart from the common faults that occur with the back somersault (tucked), which apply equally to the piked and straight versions, the back somersault (piked) may lack rotation due to the failure of the performer to assume a tight pike after take-off. The most common fault in the straight back somersault is the failure to achieve sufficient height and to maintain sufficient body tension, in order to prevent the performance of a low and hollow-backed somersault.

59.

56–9. Straight back somersault. Having initiated a strong lift into the somersault, Paul Burgoine snaps his arms down to his sides in order to assume a perfect, straight body position throughout the technique.

37

60.   61.   62.

'Lazy' Back Somersault (Straight Three-Quarters Back Somersault to Front Drop Landing) (Plates 60–6)

The take-off for this technique is similar to that for the straight back somersault, except for the fact that less hip lift is required in order to complete only a three-quarters rotation. As the performer has executed a quarter rotation (90°), the arms remain static and allow the body to catch up so that the performer achieves a perfectly straight position, with the arms being carried straight down at each side. At a position where just over half a somersault (180°) rotation has occurred, and the performer has a clear sight of the bed, a very slight piking of the body may occur in order to adjust for a safe front drop landing. Immediately prior to landing, the arms are swung forward and the knees are bent in order to assume safe

front drop contact with the bed. Once again, as with 'crash dive', this is a slightly more advanced technique which requires a good degree of control and confidence. Therefore, it is advisable in the early stages to learn this stunt using either a spotting belt or crash mat, or both.

Common Faults. Once again the normal faults that occur in the back somersault, especially the straight back somersault, apply to the three-quarters back somersault. The most dangerous fault that can occur is the initiation of too much rotation, coupled with a hollowing of the back caused by lack of body tension and control. As this fault can lead to injuries of the back, it is vitally important for the crash mat or spotting belt to be used in the early stages of learning, in order that the correct amount of rotation and body

38

63.   64.   65.

tension can be achieved in safety.

Twisting Somersaults

Having mastered the basic somersaults the next stage, as for the fundamental exercises, is to add varying amounts of twist. There is no doubt that the technical performance of twisting somersaults produces the greatest source of argument within the world of trampolining. There are many different methods of initiating twists within somersaults, as there are different types of performers, although there are only three methods which are mechanically recognized: 'twist from the bed'; 'action/reaction'; 'torque twist'. Because this area would require a great deal of technical analysis, we have chosen to illustrate a few of the twisting stunts and provide only an outline of their

66.

60–6. Lazy back somersault. Erica Phelps displays perfect 'form' throughout the execution of this technique. Note, in plate 64, the slight piking at the waist in order to speed up and adjust the amount of rotation in preparation for the front drop landing.

39

67.

68.

performance, in the knowledge that, at this stage, the performer should have the services of a competent coach who would provide any necessary technical details.

Barani (Front Somersault, Straight, with Half Twist) (Plates 67–71)
The Barani is, essentially, a forward somersault in the straight position, where the performer never loses sight of the bed, resulting in the execution of a half twist. It is vital to emphasize that the performer's intention should initially be upon the take-off, which is as for a somersault in the straight position. The twist should come, primarily, as a result of the head action. If emphasis is placed upon the twist then, at best, the action will be performed in a deeply piked position or, at worst, will result in an uncontrolled 'cartwheeling'

action. The take-off is initiated in much the same manner as for a piked forward somersault except that a strong heel-lift is implemented to prevent any piking at the waist, enabling the body to remain straight throughout the rotation. The take-off should be much stronger and higher than for the piked somersault. The head is held high throughout the technique, and with the eyes focusing upon the centre of the bed, whilst the arms are brought down to the sides of the body in order to aid the twisting movement. It may be noted that, in the photograph, the performer has chosen to twist to the right and, therefore, the right arm is brought into the body slightly quicker than the left. It is the combined action of the head and straight arms that have provided the twist. The direction of twist is usually dictated

69.

71.

70.

*67–71. Barani. This series of photographs demon-
strates, more than words ever can, the correct
technique for the Barani. Notice that Allison Stuart's
eyes are focused upon the bed throughout the
complete movement.*

by the preferred direction of performing a
full-twisting straight bounce, although it
is our experience that some performers Barani in the opposite direction
to what seems to be their preference.

Common Faults. Two common faults can
often be observed in the initial performance of the Barani. The first results
in an uncontrolled cartwheeling action,
due to a turning of the shoulders, for a
premature initiation of the twist, before
the feet have lost contact with the bed.
The second results in a low and fast
rotation, often with the legs becoming
untidy or tucked up; this is caused by a
failure to achieve the necessary height,
often because the head and shoulders are
thrown downwards as the body lifts into
the somersault.

41

72.

73.

Rudolph (Front Somersault, Straight, with One-and-a-Half Twists) (Plates 72–7)

This technique is initiated in exactly the same manner as for the Barani, with the majority of emphasis upon performing a forward somersault with the body held perfectly straight. The arms are held much wider than for the Barani, in order to aid the speed of the twist which is to follow. Although there is a tendency to commence the twist by turning the head and shoulders immediately prior to losing contact with the bed, this temptation should be resisted as much as possible. As soon as the body has reached a horizontal position (90° rotation), and with the head looking towards the bed and causing a Barani action to commence, the left arm (in a right twisting action) is

brought sharply down towards the knees, and both arms wrap firmly against the chest to speed up the twist. This arm action causes a rapid twisting action to occur; it should be noted that the twist is executed at the highest point of the somersault, and with the performer facing towards the centre of the bed. With experience, the performer will 'spot' the bed throughout, and will consciously 'check' the twist by taking the arms out to a wide position in preparation for a perfectly controlled landing.

Common Faults. Apart from the usual mistakes that occur in the normal somersaulting technique and in the Barani, the most common fault is to treat the one-and-a-half twists as two separate movements—Barani with an extra full

74.

75.

76.

77.

twist added. It is important to emphasize that the one-and-a-half twists are performed in one movement, and with the body held perfectly straight throughout; therefore no movement at the hips should occur once the twist is initiated.

72–7. Rudolph. Brian Phelps, former British Trampoline Champion and Olympic Medallist for Diving, executes a perfectly controlled Rudolph. Notice the initial wide arm position in preparation for setting up the twist. In this movement, the action of the arms in initiating, maintaining and stopping the twist can be easily observed.

43

78.   79.   80.

Back Somersault, Straight, with Full Twist
(Plates 78–81)
The take-off for this stunt is exactly the same as for a back somersault (straight). As the feet lose contact with the bed a slight turn of the head and shoulders is initiated in order to start the twist; this occurs before the body becomes horizontal (90° rotation). The initial part of the somersault is much like a half turn into a crash dive but, obviously, with a greater amount of rotation, and a stronger and faster lifting action of the left arm, initiating a twist to the right. Having initiated the twist, and with the body held under tension, both arms are pulled into line with the body in order to accelerate the twist. Once again the performer is able to 'spot' the bed throughout the twist, and extend the arms out sideways to halt the twisting action prior to landing.

Common Faults. Once again, the normal somersaulting mistakes apply. It is quite common, however, for the performer to lose body tension when thinking of initiating the twist. It should be emphasized,

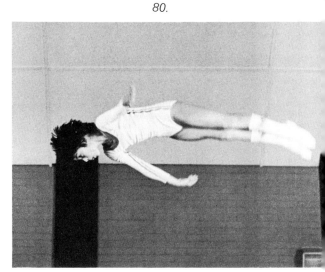

81.

once again, that the straight body position must be maintained if the full twist is to be successful.

78–81. Back somersault, straight with full twist. Having initiated enough rotation for a straight back somersault, Allison Stuart executes a complete full twist during the peak of her lift. Note the excellent body tension throughout.

82–8. Back somersault, straight, with double twist. Similar in execution to the single twisting somersault, a faster and stronger 'wrap' of the arms provides for the execution of a double twist.

44

.

83.

84.

85.

86.

87.

88.

Supporting Techniques

Safety, especially in the learning of somer-saulting techniques, is of paramount importance. Reducing the element of risk enables the trampolinist to concentrate more readily upon the intricacies of the technique which he wishes to learn. Such concentration aids success which, in turn, produces confidence, and enables the learner to progress quickly and efficiently towards a higher standard of performance. Learning somersaults is not a matter of reading or listening to advice, and then 'having a go'. Like the eternal optimist who, having jumped off a tall building, was heard at every floor to mutter 'So far, so good!', the trampolinist will inevitably come to grief unless he is able to predict the results of his efforts, and take the necessary precautions in cases where he is unable to make such predictions.

Essentially, there are three major sup-porting techniques which should be employed in the learning of somersaults. The first, the 'spotting rig', in the hands of a proficient coach, is without doubt the safest of all. The rig consists of a belt, which goes around the performer's waist, and a system of ropes and pulleys which attach to the ceiling immediately above the centre of the trampoline. The belt itself comes in two varieties, one which sup-ports only somersaults, and one which will support twisting somersaults. Although the spotting rig may seem to interfere with the performer's arm action in some techniques, this is more than com-pensated for by the knowledge that very little can go wrong which will endanger the performer himself.

The second supporting technique is provided by manual assistance, where the performer is actually being supported by another person who is standing, or bounc-ing, on the trampoline (plates 89–91). The type of support given depends entirely upon the existing skill of the performer and the technique to be performed, ranging from a firm grip on the performer's clothing, or a towel secured around his waist, to the light placing of a hand in preparation for aiding rotation. It must be stressed that the person doing the sup-porting must be a reasonable trampolinist himself, and must have received adequate instruction and experience in supporting techniques. It should also be stressed that, where possible, manual supporting techniques should be used only after the stunt has first been performed, with some success, in a spotting rig, and the per-former has been deemed capable of progressing.

The third technique involves the use of a 'crash mat', a large and thick foam mat-tress (plate 92). This is usually employed after the performer has achieved contin-uous success with the other supporting

89–91. Manual support for the back somersault. Realising that his performer is experienced in the back somersault, Brian chooses merely to place his hand against her hips in order to provide additional rotation if and when it is required. He is ready at all times to catch the performer should anything go wrong. As soon as he feels that the performer no longer requires his assistance, he will progressively remove his support.

92. Safety aids. The combined use of the overhead spotting rig and the crash mat, when correctly used, provides for perfect safety no matter what dif-ficulties the performer might find himself in. It should be noted that the crash mat is physically pushed onto the trampoline immediately the per-former has left the bed and is entering into the desired technique.

92.

90.

91.

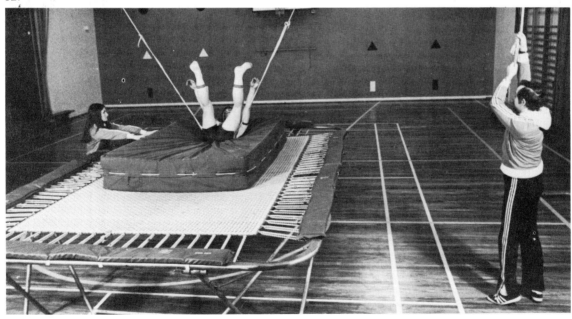

Trampolining

techniques. Once the performer has left the bed, and is entering into the performance of a technique, the crash mat is quickly slid onto the trampoline, in order to provide for a soft landing should any mistake occur. The crash mat may also be used in conjunction with the spotting rig, especially in cases where the technique to be performed is of an advanced nature.

Routine

The following is a routine involving basic somersaults, the performance of which would qualify the trampolinist for the Elementary Gold Award of the British Trampoline Federation.

10 Contact Routine
1   Back somersault (straight)
2   Piked straddle jump
3   Back somersault (tucked) to seat
4   Half twist to feet
5   Piked jump
6   Front drop (piked)
7   Through to back drop
8   Half twist to feet
9   Tuck jump
10   Front somersault (piked)

CHAPTER FOUR

Multiple Somersaults and Advanced Variations

Having mastered the fundamentals, the trampolinist's attention now turns to the more difficult stunts, vital for competition in modern-day trampolining. The numbers of these stunts, and their complexity, can be only hinted at in a book of this size. in the past ten years the world of trampolining has progressed through several stages where tricks and routines, once thought impossible, have now become commonplace. The double somersault is now commonly performed, the triple somersault is often seen, and the aspiring trampolinist has turned his attention to the quadruple and even the quintuple (five rotations) somersault. The Fliffis, once thought to be the limit of man's ability to somersault and twist at the same time, has given way to the Triffis, and who knows what might follow that!

All these advanced movements require the same precision of balance, control and co-ordination that are required for basic exercises. Although these techniques place greater demands upon speed, skill and concentration, the need to link these stunts into a routine places an infinitely greater amount of emphasis upon experience, confidence and control.

It is only in the world of trampolining that such a complex variety of human movement can be observed. The trampoline has opened up avenues of human performance that are only now starting to be exploited by the associated sports of gymnastics and diving. It has long been realized that, in any area of human activity which places great demand upon man's kinesthetic senses, the trampoline plays an invaluable role. To this end, it has been useful to a variety of activities, ranging from ice skating to the preparation and conditioning of astronauts in the NASA space programme.

In the following pages, we have decided to illustrate in detail some of the special variations in somersaulting peculiar only to the trampoline (somersaulting from back and front drop take-off), as well as multiple somersaults with and without twists. Such a small selection of the more advanced stunts can do little more than merely whet the appetite of the more competitively minded trampolinists. It is our hope that this small sample will provoke the reader to pursue the art and science of trampolining to its very limits—whatever those limits might be!

Up until this point, we have chosen to detail some of the common faults that occur in the performance of the more basic techniques. As with everything else in life, the more complex the skill or technique is, the more that can go wrong in its execution. We have chosen to omit any comments regarding 'common faults' from this chapter, because to detail them would require more space than this book permits, and may only confuse the more inexperienced trampolinists.

Somersault Variations

As pointed out earlier, the trampoline is unique in that it allows take-offs and landings to be performed from parts of the body other than merely the hands and feet. It is possible to perform somersaults, twisting somersaults and even multiple somersaults to and from back, front, seat, and knee drop landings. In competition, however, such somersaults are more usually performed using front and back drop landings. Although we have chosen to illustrate such movements using a three-quarter front somersault to back drop landing, with front somersault out (crash dive, ball-out), and three-quarter back somersault to front drop, back somersault out (lazy back Cody), it should be noted that there are many other methods of utilizing these landing positions, using more complex techniques. For example, in the case of the back drop landing, it is possible to perform a one-and-three-quarter front somersault to back

drop followed immediately by a two-and-a-quarter somersault, with a half twist to feet (one-and-three-quarter front, ball-out with a Barani-out Fliffis)!

Crash Dive, Ball-Out (Tucked) (Plates 93–101)

Having executed a normal crash dive (see *page 32),* the performer lands in a normal back drop position with the legs being held straight, at an angle just short of 90°. From this position, and at the point where the trampoline is beginning to recoil, the performer kicks forward and upward by sharply extending the straight legs and unbending at the waist. Having initiated strong and high forward rotation, the legs are bent so that the body assumes a normal tucked position in order to execute the one-and-a-quarter somersaults to feet. The landing is performed in the same way as for a normal front somersault.

The performer may 'lead up' to a ball-out to feet by executing a strong, high and controlled back drop to front drop, with straight legs throughout the flight. This may be followed by executing a back drop tucked single front somersault to back drop or, alternatively, one-and-a-quarter somersaults to a seat drop landing. At this stage he may then choose to enter into the first back drop by means of the crash dive, and then progress towards the execution of the complete technique.

93–101. *Crash dive, ball-out (tucked). Having executed the crash dive, Erica Phelps drives forwards and upwards with her legs in order to achieve a perfectly controlled high front somersault. By looking at the pillar in the background, it can be seen that the correct action achieves little or no forward travel along the bed. This technique has been 'spotted'.*

94.

95.

97.

98.

100.

101.

102.

103.

104.

One-and-Three-Quarters Front Somer-
saults, Rudolph Ball-Out (One-and-
Three-Quarters Front Somersaults, One-
and-a-Quarter Somersaults with One-
and-a-Half Twists) (Plates 102–12)
The intention in the first part of this
technique is to perform a high front
somersault into a back drop landing. The
take-off is executed in the same manner as
for the ordinary front somersault, but with
a greater amount of lift and a stronger
action of the hips, in order to provide for
the height necessary to the increase in
rotation. Having assumed a tight tucked
position, and at the point where the first
somersault has been completed, the performer should be at the peak of his
lift. By releasing his grip upon his knees the
performer will gain a clear sight of the
centre of the trampoline. Extending into a
perfectly straight position, he executes the
next three-quarters of a somersault in
exactly the same manner as for a normal
crash dive.

52

The first part of the movement from the
back drop position is executed in much the
same manner as for the normal ball-out,
except that the drive of the legs is much
stronger, in order to be able to achieve the
next one-and-a-quarter somersaults with
the body extended in a perfectly straight
position. The first quarter of the somersault sees the performer rotating upright
into a straight position, where he will gain
sight of the trampoline. From this point
onward the Rudolph (front somersault
with one-and-a-half twists) is executed in
the normal manner (see page 42).

102–12. One-and-three-quarters front somersaults,
Rudolph ball-out. Having achieved the necessary
height and rotation, Brian executes a superbly
controlled exit from the tucked into the straight
position in preparation for the back drop landing.
Plates 105–7 on their own would represent a normal
crash dive. The drive into the Rudolph must be
strongly executed in order to provide for the straight
body rotation which is to follow. With the height
which he manages to acquire, the execution of the
Rudolph becomes almost incidental.

5.

106.

107.

108.

109.

0.

111.

112.

113.   114.   115.

116.   117.   118.

119.   120.   121.

Lazy Back Cody (Plates 113–21)

The first part of this technique is executed as a normal three-quarters back somersault in the straight position, to a front drop landing (see page 21). As the performer is entering into the front drop position, the legs bend at the knees as if attempting to kick the heels against the seat. From the front drop position, a strong push of the arms, combined with a sharp extension of the lower legs, will result in the performer rising through the first quarter (90°) of the next somersault with the body being held in a perfectly upright position, and with the hips pushing forward in order to execute the back somersault which is to follow. From this upright position, the performer bends sharply at the knees and waist to assume a tucked position, thus executing a back somersault. The landing is achieved by extending at the waist, at the point where the performer spots the bed, much in the same way as for a normal back somersault.

The performer may first learn to execute the Cody technique by practising a front drop and, using the correct leg kick, carry this straight through to back drop whilst maintaining a straight or slightly hollowed body position, piking at the last minute for the back drop landing. He may then enter

113–21. Lazy back Cody. The execution of a high and controlled three-quarters back somersault to front drop is followed immediately by a perfectly timed push of the hands and kick of the legs in order to achieve the height and rotation for the one-and-a-quarter back somersaults which follow. Allison Stuart has achieved so much height in her Cody that, once again, she demonstrates a perfect 'out' position in preparation for her landing. This ensures that she can perform the next technique with complete confidence and with perfect control.

into the technique by using the lazy back, but he should ensure that satisfactory safety precautions are enforced to guard against the greater rotational force provided by this entry—by using either a spotting rig, a crash mat, or both.

Double Somersaults

When the performer has reached the stage where he can begin to think in terms of multiple somersaults, he is also entering a phase in his trampolining career where he will begin to look forward towards competition of the highest calibre. The performance of multiple somersaults marks his progression towards a new dimension of trampoline techniques, the complexity of which would have astounded the early acrobats, and the limitations of which can, at this time, only be guessed at. The performance of multiple somersaults requires the highest degree of courage, skill and control demanded of the performer up to this point. As pointed out earlier in this book, backward rotation affords the performer a clear view of the bed immediately prior to landing, and is thus regarded as the easiest type of rotation for the purpose of safety in execution. It is for this reason that the double back somersault is the most commonly performed multiple somersault in competition, and therefore we choose to illustrate the technique in this section.

It is important to note that the performer must be able to control the performance of single somersaults in swing-time, and with exceptional height and faster initial rotation. He must also be able to perform a very high and controlled layout backward

55

122.

123.

somersault. The initial practice for all multiple somersaults should be performed with the aid of an overhead spotting rig.

Double Back Somersault (Tucked) (Plates 122–6)
The initial lift for this technique is provided in exactly the same manner as for the backward somersault (straight), using a strong thrust of the hips and lifting action of the arms, in order to provide for the increase in height and rotation. The body thus commences the technique in a fully extended position and, only when having lost contact with the bed, assumes a fully tucked position in order to increase the speed of rotation. If this action is correctly performed, it will result in a second somersault rotating faster than the first, and the double rotation being fully completed as the performer begins to

descend from the high point. The exit, from the tucked position, is performed in exactly the same controlled manner as for the single backward somersault.

Twisting Double Back Somersaults

Having mastered the problems of double rotation the performer, as he did for the basics, may then proceed to add varying degrees of twisting to their performance. The execution of multiple twisting somersaults (Fliffes, Triffes, etc.) places the highest demands of all upon the skill,

122–6. Double back somersault. Having initiated the very strong hip lift, in order to provide for the increase in rotation, Paul Burgoyne quickly assumes a tightly tucked position with his hands firmly grasping his knees in order to prevent the body from opening out too early. After one-and-a-half rotations (plate 125), Paul 'spots' the bed and executes a sufficiently good landing for him to follow this stunt with another technique.

124.

125.

126.

127.

courage and physical ability of any trampolinist. It is impossible to detail the number of stunts comprising varying degrees of rotation (somersaulting) and gyration (twisting). Every year that goes by sees the practice of stunts which were once thought impossible and the performance, in competition, of techniques regarded as incredible. The Barani-Out Fliffis (double front somersault with half twist in the second somersault) is commonly regarded as the 'easiest' of all the Fliffes techniques. But there are many other techniques which are regarded, by some, as now being easy. There is the Barani-In Fliffis (half twist in the first somersault); the Rudy-Out Fliffis (one-and-a-half twists in the second somersault); The Full-In, Back-Out (double back somersault, with full twist in the first somersault); the Half-In, Half-Out Fliffis

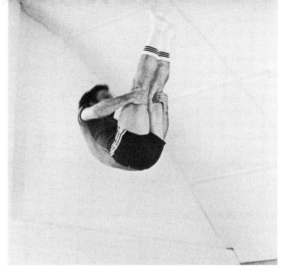

128.

(double backward somersault with a half twist in the first somersault and a half twist in the second somersault) etc., etc. Perhaps you, the reader, may one day become a trampolinist whose imagination prompts the performance in reality of a hitherto 'impossible' technique.

Barani-Out Fliffis Piked (Double Forward Somersault Piked, with Half Twist in the Second Somersault) (Plates 127–31)
The take-off in this technique is the same as for the one-and-three-quarters forward

127–31. Barani-out Fliffis (piked). With the first one-and-a-half somersaults completed, and at the highest point in his lift, Brian 'spots' the bed in order to execute the Barani with his body in a perfectly straight position. It should be noted that the landing is made easier as the performer has a complete view of the trampoline at the end of the stunt.

9.

130.

131.

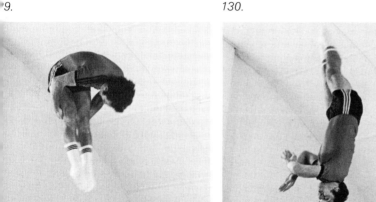

somersaults into back drop landing, or a double front somersault. The legs are held perfectly straight, and the body held in a deeply piked position throughout the first one-and-a-half somersaults. The first one-and-a-half somersaults are executed prior to the performer reaching the highest point of his bounce. It is when he reaches the halfway stage in the execution of the second somersault that the performer spots the centre of the trampoline, and maintains eye contact with the bed throughout the execution of the resulting Barani. The fact that the performer extends his body, in the execution of the Barani, results in the second somersault being slower than the first. This provides for a perfectly controlled landing in preparation for the next stunt.

'Kipping' and 'Killing' the Bed

It is common practice in the initial performances of the advanced techniques, having already achieved success in the spotting rig, to receive assistance from a coach either at take-off, or upon landing. It is impossible for the coach to provide lift to a double somersaulting technique in the same manner as he would for a single somersault (ie by 'hand spotting'). There is, however, a technique for providing additional lift to the performer which is called 'kipping'. Standing level with the trampoline bed, the coach uses his weight to depress the bed immediately prior to the performer making contact on the bounce when the technique is to be executed. The weight of the performer's own body adds to the depression already provided by the coach's body. The coach then removes his weight from the trampoline exactly at the point when the performer has further depressed the bed, which results in a recoil power equal to the weight of both performer and coach being applied to the performer alone. The resulting recoil, if timed correctly, can produce far greater height than the trampolinist might produce unaided, and thus can aid safe and successful performance during the learning stages (plates 132–8).

'Killing' the bed can be achieved by the coach adding his weight to the trampoline at exactly the same time as the performer, but remaining in contact with the bed in order to absorb all the recoil power. This technique is useful in cases where the performer is unsighted upon landing, and

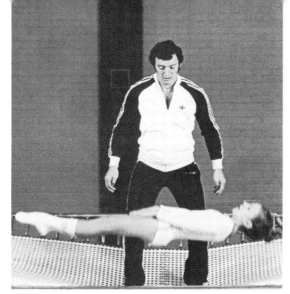

134.

135.

where further bouncing (especially if off-balance) would prove dangerous. It should be noted that the techniques of 'kipping' and 'killing' the bed should be performed only by an extremely experienced coach, and on performers who are familiar with what to expect when such techniques are used.

132–8. 'Kipping' the bed. Dropping Erica into a 'porpoise' (flat back drop), Brian provides a demonstration of the additional lift supplied by this technique. Note that in plate 134 Brian has depressed the bed, and in plate 135 has released his weight from the bed, in order to provide the added lift to achieve the height reached in plate 138. Under normal circumstances, the person 'kipping' the bed has no physical contact at all with performer.

136.

137.

138.

Trampolining

Routine

10 Contact Routine
1 Half-In, half-Out Fliffis
2 Barani-Out, piked Fliffis
3 Piked double back somersault
4 Barani-Out, tucked Fliffis
5 Tucked double back somersault
6 Rudolph
7 Full twisting back somersault
8 Double twisting back somersault
9 Forward one-and-three-quarters piked front somersaults
10 Rudolph ball-out

139.

139–42. *Competitive trampoliners.*

139. Paul Luxon, seen in action in plate 140, has been described as 'Britain's Grand Master of the Impossible'. World Amateur Champion, World Professional Champion, twice European Champion, and holder of USA, German and British National titles, he is undoubtedly trampolining's superstar, and an inspiration to all of us.

140. Paul Luxon demonstrates the need for high ceilings when performing at International level.

141. Stewart Matthews, aged 17, is three times British Champion, and displays the sort of form that ranks him second in the world, and may lead him to become only the second Briton—after Paul Luxon — to win the World Championships.

142. Authors Cyril Carter and Brian Phelps shortly after the National Superstars competition in September 1978.

143. Stewart Matthews also takes part in synchronised trampolining, with Carl Furrer. They are ranked third in the world, and are seen here with their European Gold medals.

140.

141.

142.

143.

Glossary of Terms

Trampolining, in common with many other technical sports, has developed its own language. Many of the words used in this language have been taken directly from the associated sports of gymnastics and diving, although many other terms have developed spontaneously as a result of the advanced activities practised by top performers and advocated by the leading coaches. The following are merely a few of these terms, many of which appear in this book; it is our hope that this glossary will enable the reader to enter into conversation about trampolining.

Add-on: A competive game where each performer repeats a stunt (or series) that has already been executed and adds one more of his own.

Adolph: Three-and-a-half twisting forward somersaults (first performed in competition by Great Britain's Paul Luxon, World Champion).

Arch: More often referred to as a hollow position, when the back is hyper-extended.

Axis: An imaginary line through the centre of the body about which it rotates or spins (somersaults or twists).

Back: Abbreviation for a backward somersaulting action.

Back Full: Abbreviation for a backward somersault with one complete twist.

Ball-Out: Front somersault performed from a back drop position.

Barani: Front straight somersault with one half twist where the performer does not lose sight of the bed.

Barani Ball-Out; A Barani performed from back drop to feet.

Barani-In: Multiple somersault where a half twist is performed in the first somersault.

Barani-Out: Multiple somersault where a half twist is performed in the last somersault.

Barrel Roll: see 'Roller'.

Bed: The sprung surface of a trampoline.

Blind: That portion of any stunt where the performer cannot see the trampoline.

Build Up: The controlled bounces immediately prior to the performance of any stunt or exercise.

Cast: A faulty take-off causing side to side travel across the bed due to lack of balance, usually resulting from incorrect body position.

Cat Twist: Back drop full twist to back drop.

Checking: The slowing or stopping of rotation or gyration.

Cody: Forward or, more often, backward somersaulting action performed from a front drop landing.

Corkscrew: Back drop, one-and-a-half twists with half somersault forward to back drop.

Corpse: Flat back drop, with shoulders, hips and heels landing together.

Cowboy/Cowboying: Somersaults performed in an extremely tight tucked position, but with the knees held apart from each other to enable the performer to tuck even tighter than normal.

Cradle: Back drop, half forward somersault rotation, with half twist to back drop.

Crash Dive: A three quarter front somersault performed in a straight position, with the head ducking under at the last instant so that the performer lands on his back. (This movement is usually followed by a 'ball-out'.)

Dismount: Safe method for leaving the trampoline.

Double Bouncing: Where two performers alternate their bouncing on one trampoline.

Exercise: The combination of two or more movements, usually referred to as a routine.

Feet to Feet: Any stunt, or movement, that is performed with a take-off from the feet, and a landing on the feet.

Fliffis (pl. Fliffes): Any double somersault with at least one half twist.

Flying Somersault: Any somersaulting action where the first half of the first somersault is performed in a straight, or hollow position.

Form: Appearance and style of a stunt or routine.

Front: Abbreviation for a forward somersaulting action.

Front One-and-Three: One-and-three-quarter forward somersaults from feet to back drop.

Full In/Full Out: Any multiple somersaulting action where a full twist is used in the first somersault (in), or in the last somersault (out).

Gain: Movement forward away from the centre of the bed, during the execution of a stunt, in the opposite direction to any rotation.

Half-In: Any multiple somersaulting action (usually backwards) where a half twist is performed in the first somersault.

Hand Spotting: Any assistance given by the coach or supporter with his hands.

Hollow: See 'Arch'.

Kaboom: Back somersaulting action performed from a 'flat' back drop take-off where the heels contact the bed immediately after the back to supply rotation.

Kick Out: Extending the legs and body from a tucked or piked position, slowing down rotation, in preparation either for landing or to perform twists.

Killing The Bounce/Bed: Action used to absorb the rebound of the bed in order to prevent further movement.

Kip: The assisted bounce given to any performer by another person depressing the bed immediately prior to the performance of a stunt/bounce.

Layout: A straight position, where the body is fully extended.

Lazy back: Three-quarters back somersault to a front drop landing.

Move: Any one stunt or trick.

Out Bounce: Extra foot bounce at the end of a routine for control.

Trampolining

Pike: A body position with the legs held perfectly straight and with the chest in contact with the legs. The arms may be extended sideways or, alternatively, the hands may clasp the underside of the calves, or extend forwards to contact the feet.

Pucked: A loose tucked position, used for performing twists in multiple somersaults.

Pullover: Backward somersaulting action performed either from a back drop position or from a tucked position on the bed.

Randolph: Forward somersault straight with two-and-a-half twists.

Rig: See 'Spotting Belt'.

Roller: Seat drop, full twist, seat drop.

Routine: A combination of tricks/stunts performed with one following immediately after another.

Rudolph/Rudy: Forward somersault straight with one-and-a-half twists.

Set/Set Exercise: Compulsory routine given to the performer prior to competion/examination.

Short: Failure to perform the necessary or intended amount of gyration or rotation.

Spot/Spotting: When take-off and landing are performed exactly in the middle of the trampoline. Also when non-performers stand at each side of the trampoline for safety (spotters).

Spotting Belt: Safety belt either hand-held by supporters or, more often, suspended by ropes and pulleys from overhead supports (usually referred to as a 'spotting rig'). The belt itself can be specially designed to facilitate supporting of twisting as well as somersaulting type movements.

Straddle: That position assumed in the air when the body is piked but with the legs spread wide apart; usually performed from feet to feet.

Stuck: Difficulty in completing a stunt due to lack of movement or rotation.

Stunt: See 'Move'.

Swing/Swing Time: Performing a routine, or series of stunts, with no free bounces in between.

Swivel-Hips: Seat drop, half twist to seat drop

Travel: Any movement away from the desired take-off or landing point, in the same direction as any rotation.

Trick: See 'Move'.

Triffis (pl. Triffes): Any triple somersault containing at least one half twist.

Tuck: A body position with hips and knees fully flexed, the hands clasping the shins.

Turntable: Front drop, side somersault to front drop.

Twist: Gyration of the body around its longitudinal axis (imaginary line running through the top of the head down towards the feet).

Working the Bed: The correct co-ordination of the vigorous actions required to obtain maximum height without loss of control.

Wrap: When the performer draws his arms in, from an extended position, to a position closer to his body, in order to speed up twisting movement.